MY PSYCHIC LIFE

About the author

I was born during England's post-war years in a suburban Surrey cottage, flanked by the beauty of purple and lavender rhododendron bushes. Adjacent were several acres of woodland where undetonated World War II bombs were purported to be buried although, thankfully, none were ever actually discovered.

I have always had a huge passion for the spiritual side of life and later developed as a paranormal psychic reader, meeting and reading for those from all walks of life.

Fascinating and humbling evidence of a vast spiritual energy dimension has come to light which, hopefully, may give some comfort to the bereaved and anyone who has pondered what, if anything, might lay ahead once their earthly journey is complete.

MY PSYCHIC LIFE

CONTACT WITH THE OTHER SIDE

by

MARIANNE GREEN

Vanguard Press

Dedication

My gratitude and thanks go to those beloved
family members mentioned, and the world of
spirit, without whom this book could never
have been written.

Contents

Chapter One

Roots and Early Spiritual Encounters

An air of tranquillity enveloped the olde English country garden ablaze with mid-summer blossom, dappled sunlight peeping through the weeping willow trees, illuminating the nearby babbling brook flanked by golden honeysuckle bushes, their heady aroma permeating the entire surround.

Rocking gently to and fro in the ancient wooden framed swing my thoughts drift back to yester-year as the haunting melody "Take Me Back in Time" filters from the tiny transistor radio, prompting a flow of unexpected teardrops and a barrage of poignant memories, forever etched into the corners of my very soul.

Why, I mused, it seems only yesterday that innocent young girl ran breathlessly along a quiet leafy lane dreaming endlessly of an ecstatic sunshine and starlit tomorrow interspersed with heaps of fun, laughter and most importantly, 'amour' constantly fuelled by those oh, so risqué 1950s ladies' magazines all carefully squirrelled away in her cosy bedroom at home. I pondered, if only that sweet bird of youth could flutter its coquettish plumage just once again and remain ensconced in such a heavenly time warp for evermore!

Ancestry, of course, plays such a decisive role in carving out our future pathway and my ancestors were no exception when they fled their French homeland from religious persecution and settled in London's notorious East End joining many of their Huguenot contemporaries living in the Shoreditch, Hackney areas. The entire vicinity had once been a tranquil rural surround prior to the 1600s when progress intervened bringing in its wake a mass of tanning and tallow factories, fish farms, slaughter houses, brothels and breweries and later expansion of the London Docks, resulting in a larger population leading to wide-spread overcrowded slums, workhouses and disease.

Crime was rampant amidst the hotchpotch of dark alleyways and cobbled streets of the East End of London, as was prostitution, heralding the reign of the infamous murderer 'Jack the Ripper' in the Whitechapel area where my late maternal grandmother accompanied the police and detectives hunting for him, but alas, Jack was never found, in spite of identity theories ranging from a Polish refugee to a prominent member of the English royalty.

However, my stoic, hardworking ancestors were not deterred by the harsh East End backdrop, pulling themselves up from their boot strings and gradually creating a mini empire of restaurants and coffee houses throughout London. My maternal grandmother, Amelia, was a hardworking soul and also a high spirited individual eventually becoming absolutely besotted with a handsome East End bookmaker's runner, much to her disapproving parents, even arranging secret trysts with her beloved Albert by climbing out of her bedroom window and shimmying down a nearby drainpipe straight into his outstretched arms. Eventually my great grandparents relented and a beautiful Amelia walked proudly down the aisle resplendent in old French lace and pearls where her handsome beau patiently awaited her hand.

The young couple later moved out to the genteel county of Surrey and resided in a country cottage, adjacent to ancient woodlands surrounded by purple and lilac rhododendron bushes, clusters of delicate sweet peas, apple and pear trees. There was also a smallholding at the rear of the garden, from which tiny squealing pink piglets escaped into the country cottage garden before rushing off to the nearby woodland, totally oblivious, of course, to the possibility of there being several unexploded World War II bombs buried deep within the extensive undergrowth!

All this a far cry from London's bustling East End, although the vibrancy of its street markets, cockney traders, corner street flower girls, colourful music halls and sing along community pubs would never be forgotten. My family also carried on the old Huguenot traditions of hat making, lace making, crocheting and rug making. I was often fortunate to be on the receiving end of such skills, wearing hand made little silk dresses with lace collars and cuffs and jaunty crochet berets adorned with pearl buttons, (no doubt inspired by London's East End royalty, the 'Pearly Kings and Queens' whose outer garments were always smothered in their trademark pearly buttons).

My mother was a feisty, strong character — just like her mother Amelia — and was also swept off her feet in her younger years by a kind, attractive, adoring beau (my father), secretly deciding to elope and marry in a 'Gretna Green' style ceremony on the Isle of Wight, persuading two complete strangers to act as witnesses. They returned the same day to their respective homes, acting as though nothing had happened until their secret was out three weeks later causing a major family upheaval, and a proposed annulment from her frantic parents, but to no avail!

The country cottage was a huge part of my early family life and I enjoyed a happy safe and secure childhood there, together with my two brothers, numerous cats, dogs, hedgehogs and all manner of wildlife.

My family fervently had an unusual and unwavering penchant for the paranormal world which resulted in many an intriguing meeting in our little cottage; friends and acquaintances would also visit for the benefit of receiving an in-depth psychic sitting with my incredibly intuitive grandmother, Amelia, whose paranormal experiences were widely known. Amelia sometimes used her ancient tarot pack, whereby shuffling the cards at great speed and arranging them in mystical patterns prior to giving her visitors past, present and future predictions. She would then read tea leaf grout formations after her guests had drunk their traditional 'cuppas', thereby reversing the cups and giving further insight into their future pathways with great accuracy.

Amelia's powerful psychic skills have helped many of her own family members. Her eldest daughter, Winnifred, had worked in the city of London for many years. One morning, as she was preparing to set off on her daily commute by rail, my grandmother frantically urged Winnifred to stay at home as she had an intensely dark feeling that something tragic was going to happen that very day, involving a train. Thankfully, my Aunt Winnifred heeded the warning, as her usual train was sadly involved in a serious crash, causing several fatalities.

As I approached puberty, my family moved from our idyllic cottage to a larger property in the far noisier, bustling end of the village where the energetic residents seemed to permanently work all hours of the day, their precious weekends permanently reserved for the upkeep of vegetable patches and prized colourful flower gardens with purple hollyhocks, huge sunflowers and wooden sweet pea wigwams always being high on their agendas. Upon arrival at our new property a next-door neighbour suddenly appeared with the daunting news that we were about to move into the 'house of ill luck' adding that much sadness and illness had beset the previous occupants. Luckily my down to earth mother was not in the slightest affected by such alarming information and merely advised the rest of the family these were all probably 'old wives' tales'!

However, during the intervening years it became very noticeable the continuous and unprecedented bouts of ill health and misfortune relating to death, family hardship and job losses, leading my mother reluctantly to there and then make further furtive enquiries about our house. She worryingly discovered that the previous occupants had endured much personal suffering culminating in the tragic loss of their precious little daughter who had horrifically burnt to death in the house, and their robust, healthy grandmother suddenly dropping dead in her bedroom one evening. She had been an adept dressmaker all her life, working mainly in the downstairs front living room where, fascinatingly, my elder brother as a young boy could often hear the inexplicable clicking of scissors, although never quite understanding the reason for this.

In my brother's later years, he often continued to visit the family home after moving to Nottingham for his work, but one particular weekend encountered an alarming experience. Upon his return to Nottingham, after a seemingly pleasant few days, he was disturbed to notice that his back was covered in mysterious, extremely sore, deep red welt marks. There was no reason for this strange occurrence and he decided to go to his local doctor for treatment the next day, but what was even more of a mystery to him was the complete disappearance of the deep welts the following morning. Upon reflection, I could only conclude that perhaps the 'house of ill-luck' had struck again, although why my brother had been its target is a mystery, since he had not lived there for several years.

There are many reasons why a person who has physically died has not crossed to the Other Side (the spiritual energy plane) and still appear to stay on the earth plane hovering around their loved ones or places that were familiar to them. Sudden death from a short illness or an accident, or for no apparent reason, can provoke a feeling of being unready to depart their earthly life and being stuck between the two worlds.

After much deliberation I decided to invite a well-known psychic-medium (a highly intuitive individual in contact with spirit) to our family home to find out the reason, once and for all, why the tremendous amount of sorrow and negativity had occurred there throughout the years. Upon arrival one winter's afternoon the psychic-medium immediately sensed a strong energy form attached to myself in the shape of a young girl who had tragically burnt to death in the house. He also mentioned that she felt very alone and unhappy, adding alarmingly, that some type of voodoo energy had been practised on me for many years and also other family members.

Hence the reason for all the negativity and sadness in our house for such a long period of time.

Thankfully, the psychic-medium eventually managed to gently encourage the young girl's energy to 'go to the light' and join her family who had crossed over there so many years ago, where she would be much loved.

Later I was left pondering whether I would, in fact, notice any particular changes within me and wondering if the little girl had actually managed to be persuaded to join her family on the Other Side. I did not have long to wait as the following evening whilst sitting at the old oak table in the downstairs front room I suddenly felt what can only be described as a powerful jolting sensation, right through my body. I also began to feel a sense of ineffable emptiness, intuitively knowing without a doubt that the little girl had just crossed over into the spiritual realms where she will, hopefully, be reunited with her loved ones after all those years alone on the earth plane.

Several months went by and there certainly seemed to be a calmer more peaceful atmosphere in my home. I was then invited to a workshop given by a Mrs. Lyn Rose, a local house energy clearer and a ley line (energy line) expert, in Surbiton, Surrey a few weeks later and was curious to see how she worked. Upon her arrival in a small town hall she began showing the audience many energy clearing devices that she used, which included dowsing rods, metal conductors, small hammers and white candles. She explained how each device worked and spoke of her many years clearing properties all over the Surrey area. I felt very inspired and curious as to what she might make of my house and pick up any negative energy still lurking around, and invited her there and then to visit the property.

She duly obliged and arrived some weeks later, armed with all her energy-clearing devices, but then almost immediately and unexpectedly went outside to inspect the back garden, thereafter declaring that there were two extremely long ley lines extending toward my home, veering straight upwards into the back bedroom, which was where I happened to sleep, hence perhaps the reason for my chronic insomnia for years? She mentioned that the ley lines had been affecting my energy field, also adding that spirit can actually feed off these lines, especially if there happened to be water underneath the house; this was true as my father had long ago attempted to block off a small ditch running beneath the property.

Mrs. Rose then vigorously began hammering two small metal conductors into the ground at the rear of the garden where the ley lines actually began which she stated would deflect the negativity emanating from them. She then went inside my home commenting on the amount of residual energy that had built up there, much of it negative from those who had lived there before, including energy from certain clients that I had given psychic readings. Mrs. Rose also said that she had encountered the presence of a very old lady who resembled the late Queen Mary, thereby proceeding to gently encourage the spirit to go to the light, explaining that all her loved ones would be there and that she would be much happier than remaining alone on the earth plane.

Mrs. Rose later cleansed every room in my home of any remaining residual energy and lit numerous white candles in each room ensuring that every scrap of negativity was removed; if a white candle is lit and left for as long as possible then the candle wax drizzling down its side will usually turn a grey colour which represents the clearing of any negative energy. Strangely the back bedroom, where I had so often seen spiritual sightings, and also the small downstairs hall, had appeared to contain a great deal of residual energy, so perhaps this could have also accounted for my continuous on-going insomnia and negative vibes.

Many weeks later, my home seemed to have a much-uplifted feel, leading me to believe that a more positive energy now vibrated throughout the house, especially as many work and social opportunities appeared to come my way not long afterwards.

Early spiritual manifestation

Seeing spirit can be an alarming experience initially, which is what happened to me one evening at home. I had been reading a favourite novel in my bedroom when suddenly I could sense something and upon looking up terrifyingly saw a hooded figure standing over me who, in fact, seemed to resemble a monk. At that point I shouted out to my father in an adjoining room when, unbelievably, the apparition just appeared to disintegrate into the atmosphere.

My concerned father came running in and I haltingly relayed what had occurred when he merely commented that he had often seen the monk peering over him whilst in bed, even recalling how he had seen him hovering around while out walking one day, adding that the ghost had probably come into the wrong room!

Six weeks later my father passed into the spirit world, so perhaps the monk had been some sort of a warning sign of my father's imminent passing, although I have never discovered the true answer for this spiritual visitation.

Spirit voices can sometimes be detected clearly or in a muffled tone rather like hearing radio interference. Many years ago, a shrill cackling sound was detected originating from a corner of my bedroom. Upon investigation nothing untoward appeared but still the noise seemed to be getting louder when suddenly the rasping tone of an old lady could be heard stating: "You will never ever be happy," followed by the same high-pitched cackling sound.

Two years later I happened to be visiting a friend in London who had made his name in the psychic world when he unexpectedly became aware of a very old female energy around me who seemed to have a high-pitched cackling laugh! He also stated that she had experienced much unhappiness in her earthly lifetime and had unfortunately attached to my energy field as I had been sensitive to her particular vibration.

My father was a wise old soul, far ahead of his time, always strongly believing in there being many other energy dimensions within our vast universe, often quoting the age old phrase: "In my father's house there are many mansions", and constantly holding the belief that as part of the kingdom of nature, our life cycles are repetitiously illuminated, extinguished and reignited. He was also fortunate to have witnessed several spiritual energy sightings within his lifetime.

There were many occasions when my family would sit at our old oak dining room table after having laid out tiny cardboard alphabetical squares in a circular fashion, a long-stemmed wine glass centre stage, thereafter placing our index fingers on the rim and requesting to know of any spiritual energies present. We all always firmly believed that any energies would only come through the ether to our little gatherings if they so wished and we felt extremely humbled in their presence.

Spirit would sometimes make themselves known to us by movement of the wine glass spelling out information pertaining to their previous earthly existence and describe many historical events at that time. During one such gathering an energy informed us via the glass pointing to the relevant alphabetical circular letters, that he had been a highwayman during the $14^{th} - 15^{th}$ century holding rich coach occupants to ransom, and another entity fascinatingly and falteringly described how he had existed in the 1700s, working in a London tavern, sleeping on straw matting, with little food or water.

A particularly memorable instance was when a spirit imparted some personal information specifically to me, advising that I would meet a life partner from the York area of England, and I would have three children. Several years later spirit's message did come to fruition, only sadly not to me, but to my younger brother who had been sitting aside me at the time of our gathering, so perhaps there had been a spiritual mix up, or even spirit playing games at that time!

One of my very first experiences of spiritual energy happened when my grandmother, Amelia, passed into the spiritual realms after suffering a very painful duodenal ulcer. My family and I were naturally overcome with grief at her passing and on the morning of her funeral I had been resting on my bed thinking of her (I was just seventeen years of age), when suddenly several extremely bright white lights appeared along the inside of the bedroom door which just seemed to hover momentarily before completely disappearing. I immediately called my mother and told her exactly what had occurred when all she calmly stated was, "Oh, that was probably your nan sending you a shower of stars to let you know that she is all right"! This was certainly one truly sentimental spiritual sighting that has remained constantly with me throughout my lifetime and which I shall never forget.

Another unexpected encounter happened a few weeks after my father had passed into the spirit world. One particular night, again suffering from my on-going insomnia, I was lying awake in the front upstairs bedroom at home, (the bedroom, in fact, being that of my late parents) when during the early hours of the following morning I suddenly felt the bed depress as though someone had sat on it, but upon gingerly looking around, nobody was there — the bedroom being quite light as it was mid-summer. Several minutes later the bed returned to its normal position and I slowly arose to search the house, but found nothing out of place, leading me to believe that whoever or whatever it was had paid a surprise visit from the spiritual dimension.

The following night, exactly the same occurrence happened, but this time I felt something grip around my waist for several seconds as I was lying on my side and then let go. Of course, I was terrified and unable to move, but again, upon arising and searching the house, everything was in its usual place.

Thereafter, I endeavoured to forget about the disturbing instances, only to experience a similar scenario the following week, when once more I was gripped around my waist but this time, I managed to find the strength to ask who, or what, it was. I then heard a deep-toned voice stating, "I am a friend of Delia

Sainsbury," and then, what literally shook me to the core, was my right hand suddenly being gripped tightly and then released. I instinctively reached out in an endeavour to find out more and, alarmingly, felt what can only be described as a bony skeletal hand. I quickly pulled away and just lay there absolutely beside myself with fear, when several minutes later the bed was as before, leaving an air of utter stillness within the room.

I could never understand why these strange frightening occurrences had happened, until the winter of 2013 when my father's younger brother, Victor, a healthy, witty, ninety-six-year-old, happened to reminisce about his own childhood whilst living in a small cottage in the Surbiton area of Surrey. He began describing some of their close-knit community and mentioned a family of six lively girls who lived opposite called 'Sainsbury' adding the eldest daughter, Delia, had mysteriously died in some kind of accident, but no one ever found out the exact details and if anybody else was involved in her death. Immediately I could not help but think that 'my' Delia Sainsbury, might, in fact, possibly have been one and the same lady, or could this all have been just a striking coincidence? Perhaps I will only find out when it is my turn to cross to the Other Side!

Chapter Two

Unidentified Flying Objects

Throughout my lifetime our magnificent universe has never ceased to amaze, especially when I look up at a vast star-studied night sky illuminated by moonlit rays and a twinkling milky way, which always enhances my long-held belief that we cannot possibly be the only energy housed within this huge arena.

Unidentified flying objects, or U.F.O.s have always conjured up a sense of mysticism and curiosity, together with a certain scepticism at the possibility of there being existing extraneous life-forms, albeit more advanced than our own, sharing the endless cosmos. Ancient stone carvings depicting alien flying ships and spacemen, together with startling detailed facts of the Sirius star and other enhanced planetary knowledge all mysteriously connected to the Dogan tribesmen in Mali, West Africa, have constantly fuelled speculation of a superior life force once visiting the earth plane. There were also the sophisticated advanced cultures of ancient Egypt, Greece, Babylonia and the Roman Empire, all intensifying this long-held belief, particularly when our ancestors were mere cave-dwellers at the time these highly advanced civilisations were in existence.

One of the most famous U.F.O. global sightings happened in 1947 at Roswell, New Mexico when an unusual blue light was seen in the early morning hours and a purported flying disc landing on a nearby ranch, together with other mysterious debris, which was all gathered up later by the 509th Bomber Group and flown to Carswell Air Force Case in Texas. At the same time one hundred miles away another flying disc was detected that had apparently crash landed, revealing four small alien bodies with slanted eyes and unusually shaped large heads; once again, the same Bomber Group recovered all the debris and the foreign bodies and took them to Carswell Air Force Base. The civilians who had witnessed the aliens and the debris were allegedly forbidden to mention any of their findings.

Shortly afterwards a press conference was arranged at the Air Force Base where the incidents were played down as 'just a weather balloon', although it was later stated that the purported deceased aliens were subject to stringent autopsies!

During 1976 a cattle farmer in Columbia was relaxing at his farmhouse but soon had to brave the violent storm which had erupted and hurriedly walked towards his nearby cowsheds when he witnessed a large illuminated raft hovering above and continued to watch as it landed, not believing his eyes when four small aliens suddenly emerged from the craft appearing to have protruding eyes and unusually shaped faces. The farmer, recalled entering the object, although later could not remember what happened or how he had managed to find himself outside of the craft. The only evidence of his astounding encounter were burn marks on the ground where it had landed, but the explanation for the farmer's extra-terrestrial incident still remains an unfathomable mystery to this very day.

During my early twenties there was one outstanding event that will always remain in my memory. One star-lit night in 1960 I had just returned home after an enjoyable evening with my fiancé and as we were sitting in his fashionable mini car, we were startled to see in front of the adjacent houses an extremely brightly lit large round silver object with flashing blue and silver lights underneath. It appeared to be slowly and quietly descending and hovering above the rooftops of the aforementioned houses, the area behind the buildings being open farmland. At that point several of the local residents came out to see what was happening and stood in amazement at what could clearly be seen as some type of spacecraft which continued to hover silently for several minutes, the coloured lights still flashing, but nothing appeared to exit the spacecraft. A few moments later we watched in awe as the craft suddenly slowly began to ascend and then completely disappear into the night atmosphere, leaving everyone stunned at what had just occurred. Nobody ever reported the incredulous spectacle, perhaps afraid of ridicule in our village, but in hindsight I so wish now that one of us had had the courage to report there and then this unique incident.

In the month of September 2012 I was walking home one quiet evening and admiring the overhead star-filled night sky when a huge bright orange-coloured round object could be seen, which a passer-by also had detected and remarked, "Are you looking at what I've just seen in the sky, I believe it's a U.F.O.!" We both stopped and continued to watch the slow-moving orange object as it began to descend on nearby fields, which strangely, had been the scene of the aforementioned spacecraft siting all those years ago. The passer-by then started excitedly gesturing to other people who had begun gathering in the street peering upwards at the unusual orange object which could now be clearly detected as some type of spacecraft and not, as was earlier mentioned amongst the crowd, 'one of those Chinese lanterns'. At that point no sound emanated from the object and we continued to watch as it began slowly ascending and silently gliding away into the distance until disappearing completely into the night sky. I then hurriedly bade farewell to the other observers still standing there in amazement and rushed home determined on this occasion to report the incident to the local constabulary, who appeared to be extremely interested and stated that they would endeavour to investigate the entire area for further sightings. However, several weeks elapsed and disappointingly, nothing further was ever mentioned of this incredible sighting.

Chapter Three

Electro Magnetic Energy
and
Further Spiritual Evidence

Energy, a truly vital power house for our physical and emotional well-being, prompts huge surges of motivation, passion and exhilaration to debilitating low mood swings and physical health incapacities. Our energy body known as the 'aura', comprises multi coloured vibrational layers described as the Etheric, Emotional, Mental, Astral, Higher Etheric, Celestial and Ketheric. It connects out to the vast spiritual energy dimensions and can also expand or shrink according to one's energy level, i.e. an elderly person's aura can sometimes reduce whereas a child's stronger aura can actually enlarge. Scientists have confirmed that the aura does actually exist and approximately fifty years ago 'Kirlian' photography, a method of photographing energy radiating from living objects, was developed by two Russian individuals named Semyon and Valentiana Kirlian. They discovered that when photographing a leaf which had been cut in half its etheric energy field would appear. Several well-known healers' hands have also been photographed whilst working on clients and the energy coming from the finger-tips of the healers appeared brighter and stronger than when not working. We can also have our aura photographed showing the varying dominant coloured layers of our surrounding energy field, although these can alter daily according to our moods at the time, i.e. a dominant red energy will depict anger, the coloured energy of green or pink a loving mood, or yellow denoting a strong willpower.

Throughout the past years I have often unexpectedly witnessed many auras. One fascinating and totally unexpected instance happened whilst I was attending a 'Mind, Body and Spirit' festival at Kempton Park in Surrey several years ago, as I was sitting at the back of one particular workshop. I happened to glance toward the front row and was amazed to see vivid white jagged outlines surrounding the head and shoulders of the people sitting there, which I immediately recognised as being their aural fields, some appearing to be incredibly bright whilst others a little less so.

Another memorable aural sighting was at a psychic workshop being held at the Aetherius Society in Parsons Green near Fulham. The talk was being given by a well-known medium, Becky Walsh, who related her many fascinating experiences and the help she had been able to give to those who had entered her psychic pathway. Midway through her talk I was amazed to detect a stunning shade of green begin to build up around her head and shoulders that extended outward to a great width and which lasted for several minutes before fading into the atmosphere, denoting her sincere and loving nature.

During October 2011 I was visiting my brother and sister-in-law at their home in Nottingham. As we were sitting in their comfy living room with a good friend, Jill, I unexpectedly began to see an energy building up around her which appeared to look like the outline of a small medium built gentleman. I continued to stare avidly at the astonishing presence that soon after started fading into the atmosphere. At this point, I quickly shouted to everyone in the room to ask if they could see what was happening, but alas, no one but myself, for some unknown reason, could detect anything at all. Yet another fascinating aural experience.

Our physical body has the same structure as the white/blue Etheric energy layer. The muddy or clear hued Emotional sphere is about our feelings, dependent on what we generate from within ourselves, and is connected to the lower Astral energy layer, i.e. where we reside after death. When mediums make contact with the spirit world it is usually this spiritual level they connect with, although there are also Guides or Ascended Master spirits who come from a higher energy sphere.

The Mental yellow third energy layer is associated with our emotions, and the pink higher Astral is to do with love, acting as a bridge between the lower and higher layers. The higher Etheric level is associated with divine will and balance, and the Celestial is all about divine love and bliss.

The ultimate Ketheric layer is connected to the Supreme Universal Energy, the God consciousness.

Energy comprises three differing types — earth, cosmic and human.

Earth Energy

Every part of Mother Nature's magnetic umbrella has an inner and outer energy field from trees, flowers, plants, a blade of grass, to stones, pebbles, etc. (simply hugging a tree will automatically strengthen the human aura). This particular energy is also used to ground, protect and balance us, especially psychics during their sittings who surround themselves with a visionary pure golden earth light.

Cosmic Energy

Cosmic energy comes from above and can be drawn down into our body as a shimmering pure white cleansing and energising light. Psychics use this in abundance throughout their readings.

Human Energy

Our inner and outer energy body is human energy which governs our lives, i.e. the way we live, interact, etc. as energy compatibility is vital for a happy and contented mind-set.

The outer aural field also links to our swirling energy centres known as the 'chakras' where two hundred and sixteen energy channels cross. These are located along our spinal cord and attract various colours corresponding to our health, i.e. the red base chakra, the orange sacral chakra, the yellow solar plexus chakra, the green-pink chakra, the blue throat chakra, the purple brow chakra and the violet crown chakra. It is mind energy that can re-energise an unbalanced chakra and just by gently blowing an imaginary corresponding colour into a particular energy centre will correct the working of such a chakra and re-energise its health benefits.

At times our energy field can become weakened and overloaded with negativity from ourselves, or from others known as 'energy transference', i.e. every thought, word spoken or written is an energy form and can sometimes result in what is known as a 'psychic attack' which can create havoc involving all manner of problems for the person on the receiving end such as illness, accidents, personal and professional problems, etc.

Several years ago, a physic attack or 'curse' was inadvertently delivered to me by way of a gentleman client, 'N', who sadly had unknowingly experienced numerous such attacks himself from not only unfriendly neighbours, but also from his beloved son, whom he clashed emotionally with and also his ex-wife who is now in the spiritual realms. My client had not been an exemplary spouse and I felt he had been rather spurious and somewhat arrogant towards her whilst she had been on the earth plane. I nevertheless continued with his psychic sitting although to my detriment, as I suffered much illness immediately thereafter, also experiencing severe and agonising mouth and gum problems for weeks which I later discovered had alarmingly been directed towards me through N's ex-wife. This was obviously a strict lesson to be more observant when reading for a client. I thereafter begged spirit for the psychic attack to be lifted and also to be forgiven for any misinterpretation that had arisen. Thankfully my request was granted soon after.

Another instance for a psychic attack can occur when a Ouija board has been used. This can sometimes attract all manner of negative entities and even poltergeist situations, which happened to a group of teenagers who had been playing games with a Ouija board one evening at the home of one of the young people. A participant found himself, alarmingly on the receiving end of the wrath of an entity in the form of poltergeist activity later that same evening. Objects were actually thrown at him whilst in his bedroom, and all the young people had nightmares and depression thereafter. A psychic-healer was called to the rescue who promptly cleared the negative energy where the gathering had been held by using several methods from prayer to smudging with pure sage and purifying with certain crystals, also cleansing the energy fields of each of the young teenagers concerned, wherein the energy lifted removing all the poltergeist activity, depression and nightmares experienced by the group, imprinting a dire warning never to touch a Ouija board again.

There are many ways, as mentioned above, to clear our energy field that I often refer to as 'energy daily maintenance', the simplest of which being to relax and breathe in an imaginary, enveloping, shimmering white, cosmic light, thereafter a protective golden light, a.m. and p.m. or just clapping hands in an anti-clockwise motion three times around yourself and then running your hands under cold water, which removes any persistent negativity. Wafting a smoking sage, rosemary or frankincense incense stick around you and placing smoky quartz, tourmaline, rose quartz or amber crystals around your working or living space will help clear negative energy, as residual energy often lingers in walls.

Spraying with a crystal essence such as Bush's 'Grey Spider Flower' will also absorb any unwanted energy or fear. Kirlian photography is a popular method of looking at our energy field (or the aura, as previously mentioned). Several years ago, tests were taken of a woman's hands whose energy field was extremely weak and the flower essence 'Vita Florum' was administered. A photograph was then taken which showed her aura becoming brighter and after three minutes her energy field was glowing again (there are also other essences which will give the same effect).

Amulets or talismans are well known as symbols of protection, especially in Greece and Egypt where they are part of everyday life. They have been in existence since time began particularly in the days of black witchcraft and are used to bring good fortune throughout our life journey and the after-life. A protective talisman can be anything from a stone, a piece of wood or a jewel and symbols are always associated with them such as the Egyptian Eye of Horus, the ankh (the symbol of life), or the Jewish Star of David.

Geopathic Stress

Have you ever gone into a room and experienced a sense of unease or felt unwell in a certain building? Well, there is a very good reason for this in the form of 'geopathic stress' which can affect our immune system and cause a host of illnesses such as loss of appetite, depression, exhaustion and insomnia. Planet earth has a powerful surrounding electro-magnetic field to which we are all fine-tuned via our energy body, and there are a mass of energy lines running throughout our planet called 'The Hartmann grid', 'The Curry grid' and 'Ley lines'. Often ancient sites such as Stonehenge in Wiltshire, churches and burial sites are built where ley lines cross and throw out much geopathic stress, some positive or negative, especially if there is water running underneath the sites which alters the frequency of earth's natural energies.

Physical illness can be caused through disturbing earth energy lines by all manner of electrical appliances such as radios, televisions, computers, telephones, fridges, washing machines, etc. and from outside pylons, which is where a 'dowser' can help to alleviate the unwanted negative and harmful earth energy. (Dowsing maps and dowsing equipment like grounding metal copper rods are used to stem and neutralize the negative energies.) It is well worth calling in a dowser to assist in this process should your property be affected by geopathic stress. Also, a cat is usually drawn toward negative geopathic energy centres, whilst a dog will dislike them intensely!

However, a relaxed mind-set can always help us attune to earth's fluctuating energy waves, known as 'Schumann' waves and can instil healing in both our physical and energy bodies.

Further Spiritual Evidence

There have been a plethora of ghostly apparitions witnessed throughout past years including my own unforgettable sightings, one of the most memorable being that of my Spirit Guide — Guardian Angel many years ago.

One summer's night I was yet again having trouble sleeping. The bedroom door had been left ajar and light filtered from my nearby neighbour's house when upon glancing around the room I could hardly believe my eyes as there standing in front of the door was the astonishing figure of an extremely tall fair haired gentleman dressed in a long cream robe, and around his shoulder area there appeared to be small dark wings. He just stood motionless staring at me with the most incredible piercing ice blue eyes that I had ever seen. At this point, I abruptly endeavoured to awaken my sleeping partner, but upon turning back towards the figure, he had seemingly just disappeared into the atmosphere. I then ran frantically all over the house looking for signs of anything untoward, but everything was as normal, although intuitively I knew that I had just witnessed one of the most amazing personal spiritual visions and one which will never fade from memory.

A very vivid spiritual sighting occurred several years ago which will also always remain with me. Several years ago, late one autumn night, I was endeavouring to get some sleep (in spite of my ongoing insomnia), and managed to doze off in the early hours of the morning, but was inexplicably awoken shortly thereafter. My bedroom wasn't quite in total darkness as I had omitted to close the curtains properly leaving shafts of light coming through the windows. On briefly looking wearily around the room I was shaken to the core to see two eerie figures standing at the bottom of my large double bed. Naturally, I was immediately very frightened indeed, petrified being more the word, and just lay there frozen with fear thinking that burglars had entered the house. I then managed to slowly look more closely at the figures and to my astonishment, recognised one of them as being my sister-in-law's late father who had passed into spirit some years earlier. I could also detect that he appeared to be wearing a brown patterned jacket and grey trousers, and was staring very intently at me, but I did not recognise the other figure standing just behind him. My sister-in-law's father just seemed to stare at me penetratingly for a couple of seconds at which point I let out one almighty scream and shouted for help. In that instant both figures just completely vanished into the atmosphere.

After a few minutes of just laying there unable to move, I finally managed to timidly leave my bed and go nervously all around the house, looking in every nook and cranny for signs of a possible break-in, but after a thorough search, everything appeared to be intact. For the rest of the day and, in fact, for quite some time afterwards, I was still in shock from such a traumatic experience and often find myself relating what had happened that day.

Another remarkable spiritual sighting involved the comforting reassurance of an old friend's well-being from the Other Side. Gill had unexpectedly been taken to hospital and tragically passed away soon after, leaving family and friends in deep shock and absolute disbelief as only the previous week she had been sitting in her flower decked garden enjoying the summer sunshine, laughing and joking with her partner and daughter, seemingly in very good health. After Gill's passing into the spiritual realm I was sorting out my clothes in a front upstairs bedroom in preparation for her funeral reminiscing about all our time together when I suddenly saw a very large vivid grey flower (a shade of grey that I had never seen before) quickly dart from floor to ceiling in front of me. I realised instantly that this was her way of letting me know she was all right on the Other Side, especially as flowers were Gill's trademark, her house and garden often resembling the Chelsea Flower Show!

The second reassurance of Gill's well-being in the spiritual realms happened again in the upstairs front bedroom of my house which had happened to be her favourite room. It was late in the evening and I was still wide awake in a back bedroom, when I suddenly felt compelled to go into the aforementioned room. Upon entering, I could hardly believe my eyes, as there, standing large as life in front of me, was Gill looking very well, and amazingly, wearing her favourite black and white herringbone coat. Spirits communicate through telepathy, but she did not appear to relay any messages, only to just stand there staring. I then went joyously towards Gill in greeting but unfathomably discovered my outstretched hand literally going right through her, at which point I felt a tremendous jolt go through me and then found myself back in my own bed. This I felt was a truly alarming but unique and incredible experience and I appreciate how wonderful of Gill to have let me know that she was indeed 'alive and kicking' on the Other Side.

Our physical and subtle energy bodies are attached to an invisible cord which has often been detected by those who inexplicably have found themselves outside of their physical body. This usually happens during sleep state or meditation and as long as this cord is connected to our physical body, we are still physically alive. A floating sensation occurs allowing a different surround to be reached in seconds and is often described as 'an out of body experience' or 'astral travelling'.

Several years ago, a friend's aunt had unexpectedly been admitted to hospital suffering with heart problems. She was taken to the operating theatre but tragically had clinically died for a few minutes. However, the lady had against all odds, been revived and upon waking related an astonishing experience to the hospital staff concerned. This was a 'no nonsense' type of an individual who had always believed wholeheartedly that physical death was the absolute end for us all, brushing aside any talk of an after-life as sheer and utter nonsense! However, upon her return to the recovery ward she later informed the staff there of having found herself floating up to the ceiling and actually watching the surgeons frantically working on her body, thereafter hearing them pronounce that she had gone, before feeling what could only be described as a massive jolt and discovering that she had, in fact, returned to her physical body laying there on the operating table. The lady in question soon after learnt that the operating staff had been aware of many, many similar cases, but had always been advised not to mention these to anyone. Since her startling experience my friend's aunt has become a staunch believer in life after death, and is purported to broadcast her amazing experience in no uncertain terms to any 'doubting Thomas' who crosses her path!

There was a very famous 'out of body' case which happened to a gentleman called Sylvan Muldoon when he was just twelve-years-old. He was staying with his mother at a spiritualist retreat and fell asleep early one evening, but awoke with a strange feeling of being actually stuck to the bed thereafter sensing his body vibrating and hearing buzzing sounds and pressure in his head. He then opened his eyes and was astonished to see that he was actually floating horizontally just above the bed and moving toward the ceiling. He then found that he could move around very quickly and glide through doors and walls and amazingly he had x-ray vision. He left his bedroom and then tried to awaken those in the next room only to discover his hands passing straight through them. After moving around the house for several minutes suddenly he felt a tremendous jolt to his body and awoke instantly and found himself back on his bed.

I have also experienced several 'out of body' experiences myself, one such instance happening during the autumn of 2015 when I found myself leaving my bedroom and floating downstairs toward the large front room of my home. Upon entering the room, I was overjoyed to see my late mother, Marjorie May sitting on the flowery sofa looking much younger with a dark-haired older lady whom I did not recognise. At that point I remember going toward my mother and endeavouring to hug her only to alarmingly discover my hands going right through her, all the while my mother sitting motionless and just appearing to stare ahead of her. The room was also vividly lit in a bright white light. I desperately attempted to relate to my mother how much she had been missed when suddenly I found myself floating out of the door and upstairs back into my bedroom.

The spiritual community often make their presence known in a variety of ways and one inexplicable sighting of spirit happened to another 'no nonsense' individual who was a family friend. This particular

Welsh lady was a staunch advocate of 'you only live once' and 'there being no such thing as life after'. She had suffered much physical and emotional pain throughout her sixty-five years, having overcome illness and losing her beloved husband to cancer, also losing her closest and dearest friend. However the lady soldiered bravely on truly believing that she would never see her husband or close friend ever again until, that is, several months after her husband's death when she experienced such an incredulous chain of spiritual happenings it has completely and utterly reversed her previous 'no life after' unquestionable belief.

Six months after her husband's passing she had, as usual, meticulously ensured that everything in her home was locked securely and switched off including every single electrical appliance, before retiring to bed; this was a nightly ritual as living alone had made her even more aware of safety issues. She was however, awoken one particular night, only to discover that the computer in her bedroom had inexplicably switched itself on, but even more startling was the fact she could clearly see the face of her late husband on the screen. The lady could not believe what she was witnessing. Jumping out of bed to turn the bedroom light on, the image of her husband's face was still vividly displayed on the computer screen for several minutes before the screen went blank She was totally dumbfounded, although overjoyed to have seen her beloved husband, and even more amazed to witness this strange happening every week thereafter for two whole months until she finally said a silent prayer for it to stop as it was causing her much distress.

From that moment on she was both saddened and relieved to find that such an event never occurred again, although these startling sightings have firmly changed her opinion forever that, without a shadow of a doubt, there is definitely life after death, although thought what an unexpected and incredulous way to find out!

Throughout the county of Surrey there have been a plethora of spiritual sightings, many unreported for fear of ridicule. However, there was one well-known outstanding ghostly manifestation that has stood the test of time which occurred just after World War II. A van was travelling toward the Cobham area of Surrey one rainy evening and shortly before midnight, as the driver entered an area called Tartar Hill, he happened to see a girl at the roadside signalling him to stop. As he pulled to a halt, he opened the side door and signalled to her to come in out of the rain upon which she entered the vehicle and sat down without uttering a word appearing to just look fixedly straight ahead. The young girl looked pale with a somewhat vacant expression in her dark eyes at which point the driver began to feel an inexplicable fear creep over his body but continued silently driving into Cobham High Street until stopping thinking that she may want to get out of his van.

However, the girl continued to just sit staring ahead and he then began to turn down a narrow side street called Church Street where the nearby ancient church clock happened to be striking midnight when inexplicably the van engine just cut out, the vehicle chugging to a complete halt At this point the young lady just opened the door handle and silently got out, grabbing his coat to protect herself from the heavy rainfall before scurrying away throughout the churchyard toward a house on the far side of the area. The driver sat in a state of complete surprise at what had occurred wondering who exactly the strange young female was, before moving toward the ignition several minutes later, discovering that the engine started up without any difficulty at all and then continued toward home.

Later the following week the van driver decided to investigate the matter further and visited Church Street once more making his way to the house that the young girl had been hurrying toward. Upon knocking on the door, a well-dressed older gentleman opened it and the driver explained what had occurred, also adding that he was there to retrieve his coat that she had taken. The gentleman merely smiled stating, "So, you've seen her too, you're not the first, my daughter died in a fire in this house ten years ago, she had been out with friends to The Tartar pub and came home later than she should have. It was the time we had the electricians here and we had no power that night, so she took a candle up to her bedroom, she must have been reading in bed and fallen asleep and something knocked the candle over. It was the smoke that killed her!"

The van driver then said how sorry he was and the girl's father surprisingly exclaimed that he would show him his daughter's grave, adding, "We had her buried just over there so she would still be near," and stopped at a well-tended grave surrounded by colourful flowers. The van driver then detected his coat that the young girl had taken laying on the gravestone. At that very moment he felt a slight breeze and noticed the nearby trees begin to rustle and the ancient church clock chiming out. He then startlingly felt something touch his arm and a quiet female voice saying, "Thank you for taking me home!"

For many years thereafter this strange occurrence was investigated but to no avail so perhaps the van driver was, for some unknown reason, meant to have witnessed this amazing spiritual sighting and to perhaps show him evidence that we really do continue on once our earthly life is complete.

Chapter Four

Psychic Sittings

As the years passed my interest in the paranormal became paramount and I attended an avalanche of psychic workshops, courses and meetings, often accompanied by my mother Marjorie May. We were fortunate to cross paths with several famous psychic-mediums of the day and I remember vividly the famous Doris Collins and the revered Joseph Benjamin. Doris welcomed us warmly into her Richmond home and related many amusing anecdotes of show business friends such as the talented Goons and the unique Frankie Howard who was a well-known comedian of that era.

On another occasion we visited Joseph Benjamin in his north London home. He had a great sense of humour and always a twinkle in his dark brown eyes. At that time, unbeknown to my mother and I, there was another visitor to Joseph's home whom we unexpectedly encountered, rendering us both speechless. He was a very well-known American film star who appeared to be quite taken with my very attractive mother, smiling broadly at her several times, before Joseph entered the room and formally introduced us. However, disappointingly, no telephone numbers were exchanged!

I gradually began to give professional psychic readings to those from all walks of life, including some famous faces of the day, one of my most memorable sittings being a mystery lady called Annie who arrived in a blacked out chauffeur driven limousine, cautiously stepping out of the car and making a very hasty retreat into my house, insisting that all the curtains were drawn. Her ultra-thin frame was accentuated by tight fitting black apparel accessorized with gold jewellery, dark hair piled glamorously askew on her tiny head with large dark glasses pushed behind her ears.

Privacy is always foremost in every client's mind especially those in the public eye, also the 'Spiritual Code of Conduct' must always be strictly adhered to, so without breaking any rules, all I will say is that Annie's resemblance to the wife of a well-known footballer, was patently obvious, hence her visit.

The psychic reading did involve many issues, such as Annie's children and their future, her own global, blossoming career and sadly her husband's playing away, causing much emotional distress, throughout which she sat quietly in my cosy old armchair with a bemused expression across her beautiful petite features. Towards the end of the sitting, I couldn't help stating the obvious regarding her true identity to which she just gave me a broad smile without commenting, after which she quickly arose, paid the fee and telephoned her awaiting chauffeur. This was definitely one sitting that will always be remembered.

On certain occasions I visit clients and endeavour to remember to always throw a protective energy around myself (i.e. an imaginary shimmering white light) but in one instance this proved not to be the case, which could have resulted in tragedy. During the client's reading, a young man appeared outside her house threatening and brandishing a knife, at which point she just gestured calmly to continue with her sitting, totally ignoring him. She stated that there had been a much worse situation recently when an arson attack had been made on her property, and merely asked if she would be moving and cutting all ties there! (Hence, a lesson for myself to always remember the protection exercise.)

During 2013 the wife of a famous entrepreneur came to see me for a psychic sitting. I didn't initially recognise the lady, but sensed that a personal financial issue was of the utmost importance to her. I also sensed much negative energy where her husband's future was concerned. Using my tarot cards, 'The Tower' was depicted illustrating an alarming complete disastrous downfall of his entire professional and personal life, feeling that much of the gentleman's business dealings were of a precarious nature, as were personal episodes relating to his younger years. I also tuned into a step-daughter living with the lady in question, which caused much distress and negativity. All this turned out tragically to be the case as the gentleman's step-daughter shared the family home, immensely disliking my client, and her show-biz entrepreneur husband eventually lost everything through shady personal and professional dealings, ending up in prison for many years to come. However, my client eventually divorced him and moved away to the West Country, remarrying very happily, where she remains to this very day.

When spirit is close it is usual to feel either a very warm or cold sensation or a tingle throughout our body. The surrounding temperature will also change dramatically, which is what transpired when I read for an old client who lived in the Weybridge area, approximately seven miles from my home. During her sitting we both experienced a distinct icy, tingly sensation and the room temperature quickly dropped indicating the presence of spirit. I then heard the name of Kathleen and her concern about her husband's behaviour — he was still residing on the earth plane. Upon relating this to my client (she was now the gentleman's only living relative) she confirmed the information, stating that she, too, had been worried over his erratic behaviour, so perhaps Kathleen had come through to help and advise his poor, concerned niece.

Another instance of spiritual presence occurred around my own family members. My late mother had tragically battled with Alzheimer's for almost twelve years and my father had loyally looked after her until she, sadly, had to have twenty-four-hour care in

Ottershaw Hospital, Surrey, where both he and I visited daily. I remember vividly one bitter cold evening when we had returned home and once indoors my father had switched on every electric and gas appliance available to their maximum capacity. However, approximately an hour later, the entire surround went icy cold and startlingly, the red-hot heat had reduced to barely nothing. We then started shivering and pacing about just to try and keep warm, when my father quietly stated, "I think this is spirit trying to warn us that your mother will be taken tonight."

His words were confirmed when a hospital call came through around five thirty a.m. advising us to return to the hospital. As we were driving there and managing to de-thaw on the way, courtesy of the car's heating system, the vehicle strangely became absolutely freezing cold, approximately twenty-five minutes later, which we intuitively knew at once was spirits' way of telling us that my mother had passed into their world. Tragically this, indeed, turned out to be the case and the exact time of her passing had been 5.55 a.m.!

Spiritual symbolic signs often appear to me prior to a psychic reading and can be a helpful link when tuning into the client's energy. A young lady from the Surrey area had a sitting with me in 2012 and as I meditated on her beforehand, reaching the 'alpha' state, which is a deeply relaxing mind-set that enables our intuitive side to flow more easily, I suddenly became aware of the word 'otter' in large black capitals and began to see the formation of a large brown otter in front of me. As soon as my client arrived I relayed what I had witnessed to which she replied, "Oh, the otter has always been my favourite animal since childhood, and I live in an area called Ottershaw where there used to be a famous restaurant called 'The Otter', which had a large sign outside with a painting of an otter!" I then fully comprehended the relevance of the symbolic signs prior to the young lady's psychic reading.

Another memorable spiritual symbolic sign was presented to me before sitting with a lovely lady from Surbiton, Surrey. As I was tuning into her, the energy of an elderly gentleman began to materialise who looked remarkably like the late Sir Winston Churchill. I could telepathically hear him expressing that he was frequently around the young lady in question, but did not give any indication of his connection to her. During her psychic sitting I relayed a description of the gentleman, to which she excitedly stated that her late grandfather had been the spitting image of Sir Winston and had always been mistaken for him wherever he went! Again, another sign from spirit how very close they are to us.

A lady from the area of Weybridge, Surrey came for a psychic sitting one September afternoon. Prior to her arrival I had been meditating and tuning in psychically endeavouring to relay any information that came through from the spiritual plane for her. As I continued to tune in, I could see the word 'lion' and pictures of lions all around her and the sentence 'she needs to ground herself'. The words 'a young soul and a free spirit' were encircling her name, along with the faint name of Helena or Elena, and with the word 'caution'.

Upon my client's arrival, the psychic reading began. I relayed the above information to her, to which she readily confirmed that, yes, she was a young soul and a free spirit. She had also been connected whilst working in Greece to a female named Elena, who was a close friend of a lady that held a lot of jealousy for my client (hence the word 'caution' around this name!). My client then excitedly exclaimed that her family name, and that of her grandmother was Lyon, and that she herself had always, for some strange reason, avidly collected pictures of lions!

In late 2014 a lady from Hampshire came to see me for a psychic reading and again I meditated and tuned into her before her arrival. After several minutes two names were vividly shown to me over and over again, one being Linda and the other, the old, traditional surname of Smith, together with much personal information for the client. As my client arrived, the energy of Linda was becoming more and more all-consuming. Throughout the entire psychic reading it became evident that Linda was the woman whom my client's husband had known for several years and had been having an affair with during that time which had caused her huge distress. Sometimes a strong energy field can, indeed, enter a psychic reading although uninvited! The name of Smith that had been mentioned several times for me to relate to my client was, in fact, a lady who had crossed over into the spiritual realm, named Rita Smith, and who had been a friend of my client whilst on the earth plane; I then again fully understood the significance of the symbolic signs given before the psychic reading.

Another memorable sitting was for a client whom I'll fictitiously call Rachel who was an attractive South American lady dressed in a smart cream-coloured trouser suit with matching silver accessories portraying an outwardly confident air. However, as soon as Rachel's reading began she was desperately endeavouring to compose herself dispelling any of her initial outward persona. I tuned in immediately to an abusive partner, sensing much physical and mental trauma throughout the past years, causing every shred of self-esteem to have been eaten away. I also sensed that there had been a parting of the waves and an overseas connection (which, in fact, was the case as her partner had since moved to Spain). However, I strongly felt that much negative energy continued to be directed toward Rachel in spite of their separation and that he, himself, had suffered physical abuse as a child from a mother figure which had caused deep-rooted hurt and anger issues throughout his life, directing much of his mixed up emotions toward any unfortunate female that happened to cross his path.

I have humbly learnt throughout the years that we are all here on this wonderful planet to learn certain invaluable soul lessons and I truly felt that poor old Rachel's first and foremost lessons were self-empowerment and self-esteem. Unfortunately, if we do not take heed of these lessons then they usually are presented to us repetitively, which had been the case throughout Rachel's lifetime, causing her to encounter similar partners and always allowing them to diminish her own power and self-respect. Sometimes a reputable psychic healer can help in such instances by clearing away any recurring energy blocks in our surrounding energy field (which is mentioned in the following chapter).

Many unusual psychic opportunities have occurred throughout my life journey. One such 'once in a lifetime' occasion happened several years ago when I was invited for an interview at a world-famous department store in Knightsbridge, London. The store had decided to enter the complementary medicine field and had heard about me through one of their regular customers, and were also planning to employ reflexologists, healers, Bach (flower and plant) practitioners and many other complementary specialists.

Upon arrival at the store I was met by a lady in charge of their beauty salon who then proceeded to

57

interview me about my psychic work, instructing me to give two readings, one being for their managing director. An immaculately dressed blonde-haired lady then strode in and introduced herself, sitting directly in front of me and gesturing that I now give her a reading there and then, her icy blue eyes never leaving my face, stating, "I don't believe a word of this, but just read for me **NOW!**"

I then mentally sent out an urgent request to my wonderful caring spiritual guide for help and proceeded with the sitting for the lady after a very brief meditation. Within minutes I was seeing a bakery in the Hackney area of London and several of her family members drew close that had passed to the Other Side. I also picked up she had suffered with a specific throat problem in her childhood and was also shown her present-day personal business ventures.

Throughout the above psychic reading the aforementioned lady never uttered a single word, but upon its completion she arose, shook my hand and expressed, "That was amazing, you've changed my opinion, welcome on board!" The lady then introduced me to several staff members, stating that there would be many famous clients for me to read for in the coming months, and I was then shown several of their newly furnished complementary medicine units, including one breath-taking room made of pure crystal.

I was, of course, ecstatic and awaited to hear about my starting date as the resident psychic-medium in the store's complementary medicine department and during the next few months they also sent me several kind messages of encouragement. However, suddenly all contact ceased without any reason whatsoever and later I disappointingly learnt through the open media that the store had decided to merge their new venture with another famous store based in Oxford Street who would use their own resident complementary medicine staff. What a shock for me after all the months of waiting, but felt, perhaps, this was not the road after all that I was meant to travel down, for some unknown reason, holding the comforting thought that spirit always know best, helping to lovingly guide us along our personal earthly path, although sometimes not always what we had originally planned ourselves!

I have been fortunate in visiting many famous landmarks during my lifetime, especially throughout the London area, many being for the sole purpose of reading for all manner of clients, including those in the public eye, ranging from the unique Chelsea Harbour area of London, Knightsbridge to Park Lane, where I gave a memorable sitting to the wife of a famous hotel chain owner who had just arrived from the Far East. The lady was an intuitive soul and sat swishing her long dark hair about her as we sat in the opulent and breath-taking environment surrounded by gold statues and jewellery of every description, but shortly after her sitting began she appeared very unsure of herself, especially relating to her emotional circumstances, even mentioning with an elaborate gesture of her hand that she would be willing to give up all her trappings of wealth to go away and settle for a quiet and peaceful life in the countryside, in a happy, loving and secure relationship. Her psychic reading continued for a long time thereafter bringing forth much heart-rending detail of her personal life which later prompted me to deeply reflect and remember the old adage: "All that glitters is not gold", and that true happiness is found going deep within ourselves to feed and nourish our soul, without the reliance on outer trappings to find the true meaning of fulfilment and contentment on our earth plane.

Another memorable sitting, was visiting a famous socialite living in a mews property just off the Harley Street area of London. She was a regular commuter between Hong Kong and the U.K. owning several fitness companies throughout Europe and was blessed with great beauty, intelligence and an unbelievable outward zest for everything in life, whom I'll call Ivana. She had recently opened a rather plush large gymnasium in the centre of Harley Street which had begun attracting the attention of several famed clients and also a prominent member of our royal household who visited the centre twice a week endeavouring to lose some of the weight he had accumulated over the past years and hopefully return to his once youthful admired physique.

Ivana much enjoyed London and was often seen in many famous London hotspots including the renowned 'The Ivy' restaurant and the exclusive 'Mayfair Arts Club' mingling with celebrity and politicians alike forever hopeful of perhaps one day attracting an adoring and loving 'sugar daddy' who would sweep her off her tiny manicured feet and give her an even more luxurious lifestyle, but most importantly, an inner contentment and peace of mind. Hence the old adage mentioned above coming to the fore once again!

Chapter Five

Karma and Past Life Phenomena

Karma originated in India from the word 'Sanskrit'; sometimes described as fate. Karma is an ancient spiritual law called the Law of Cause and Effect i.e. whatever we say, think or do is an energy force and immediately sent out into the universe, that same energy always boomeranging back to us, whether positive or negative, which is where the old adage originates: 'As we sow, so we shall reap'.

Many of our unfounded fears stem from past life situations. For example, I have always been inexplicably afraid of heights, enclosed spaces like an elevator and also deep water, which I firmly believe all trigger a past life reaction where I possibly could have suffered an accident high above ground, a drowning perhaps, or even been trapped in a confined space such as a prison cell.

As previously mentioned, family or friends in our present-day existence often return as a soul group from a previous incarnation, although usually in different guises for us to complete any unresolved spiritual lessons. There were several instances in my younger days where I had found it emotionally impossible to let a relationship go, even knowing full well that it had finished long ago, and now realise just how certain strong karmic, or past life links, can unfathomably penetrate our energy field and remain until possibly another incarnation for the emotional situation to be resolved.

There will possibly have been situations where you immediately recognise a total stranger, or unfamiliar area, which is where the term 'déjà vu' is often applied. I, myself, have experienced many such instances, one being several years ago.

A dear friend invited me to visit the old walled city of St. Malo for the first time and, upon exploring the area, I was amazed to discover that I recognised every nook and cranny of the area, even a striking, cream-shuttered house in a side street where I instantly experienced an icy cold sensation throughout my entire body and unquestionably sensed that this was where I had, in fact, resided in a previous lifetime and given birth to three children.

On another occasion during the 1990s I was asked to look after a local social club's private apartment whilst the owners were away. Upon entering the premises, I sensed a feeling of great unease and tremendous sadness, and later learnt from a local historian friend that during England's Oliver Cromwell era hundreds of Cromwellian troops had set up camp in the area where fierce battles were fought which resulted in a plethora of fatalities. I further learnt that many of these battles had taken place in the actual location of the aforementioned social club site, hence the distressing psychic sensation that I had felt.

Upon reflection, perhaps I had triggered a past lifetime where I had actually been involved in all the sadness and destruction of lives which can bring to the surface all manner of emotions.

Some years ago I was visiting the Hampstead area of London for the first time and as I began exploring its alleyways and streets and admiring its quaint and quirky properties I quickly sensed an inexplicable familiarity with the area, even intuitively knowing upon exploring a tiny alleyway near the breath-taking heathland that I had lived there in a previous lifetime and had been part of a naval family. However, I also then began sensing an urgent desire to get away from the entire area as quickly as possible and realised with a jolt that a past life traumatic memory had perhaps reared its head causing a sense of fear throughout my entire body.

There have been two occasions where I experienced tragic past life sensations which concerned the loss of two male babies resulting in overwhelming inexplicable feelings of deep grief and trauma. I decided to explore this further and after extensive research, I discovered many lifetimes ago that I had been involved in tragic, past life child traumas whilst living in Ireland where I had become pregnant but was not allowed to continue with the pregnancies. This resulted in unsuccessful abortions and my giving birth to two stillborn male babies, the traumatic memory remaining within my aura and triggering the personal sense of deep and overwhelming grief to this very day.

During the 1980s there was an unforgettable and compelling television programme exploring global past life phenomena, including two particular cases which caught my eye where again, the old adage, 'through the eyes of a child', appeared especially pertinent, the first involving the murder of a baby girl in India cruelly having had her tiny throat cut. Several years later there was a well-known report of a very young girl in America who unfathomably kept relating the story of a previous lifetime to her mother where she had lived in India, even bearing throat scars pertaining to a strange knife wound to her throat, and she could clearly recall the colour of the house she had once lived in and the name of the small Indian village.

Sometime later a local scientist heard about her mysterious recollections and gained her parents' permission to travel to India with the girl to investigate the matter further. He discovered after much research that there was, indeed, the tiny village with the exact name that she had given and upon their arrival the girl immediately recognised the house concerned saying that the outside colour had been altered. Upon knocking on the door, a woman opened it and after hastily explaining the reason he was there the young girl suddenly stated that this lady had actually been her mother, and she was later told that the outside of the property had been painted in a different colour from that before! The girl then went around the village and astonishingly immediately recognised an elderly villager saying, "This was the man who killed me!"

There was also another case described in the aforementioned television programme which involved a very young boy living in India who continually spoke of a town twelve miles from his home called Agra where he said he had once lived and had owned a shop that sold radios. He also said that he had been called Suresh and had been married to a girl named Uma and they had had two children. He incessantly claimed that he had been killed in a temple there by another young man. The television crew offered to investigate his claims and with his parents' permission they went to the town of Agra with the young boy and after much research found the purported radio shop where the boy said he had once lived, and astonishingly discovered an older lady called Uma, the wife whom he had mentioned from his previous lifetime. The boy said that things had been changed around in the shop since he was there, including some new units and the colour, which Uma confirmed to be correct. The television crew also asked him if he recognised Uma's children and the young boy instantly confirmed this, even stating their actual names, which left everyone there stunned and in complete shock, confirming once again, that this was unquestionably another outstanding case for evidence of reincarnation.

Chapter Six

More Spirit Sightings

As previously mentioned, the Other Side often make contact with us in a number of different ways, one being moving objects around your home and our finding them in completely different places from where we originally put them, which happened to a gifted psychic friend of mine who lived alone. She would often find objects of jewellery missing from her bedroom dressing table only to discover them later, puzzlingly placed in the centre of her kitchen table! Perfume or tobacco aromas are another favourite calling card of spirit, and quietly hearing our name called out when there is no one else around, or our even hearing loved ones' favourite music or songs whilst they were on the earth plane being played wherever we go, especially not long after their passing into the spiritual realm.

My late sister-in-law, Chris, had always been a fan of the reggae group, UB40, even arranging for two of their well-known chart toppers, 'Red, Red Wine' and 'Kingston Town' to be played at her funeral. Several months after Chris's passing her beloved son and his wife were invited to a social gathering whilst in South Africa and unbeknown to anyone there knowing anything about Chris the very two aforementioned songs were loudly playing as they walked into the event. Also, Chris's husband was startled to hear the same two tunes being played everywhere he visited in his home town of Nottingham soon after her passing, in cafes, restaurants, bars, etc., in fact, wherever he happened to frequent at that time, so perhaps this was Chris's way of getting her message across from the Other Side that she was not far away at all from her loved ones on the earth plane.

It can also be helpful to visit a reputable medium to make contact with a loved one in the spiritual dimension, which I did myself (psychic-mediums are renowned for being unable to read themselves for some unfathomable reason) several months after my sister-in-law's passing. A few moments into the reading Chris made contact slowly saying how close she was to all her family in spirit and here. She started speaking via the medium about a piece of green jewellery that she had given to me, which was absolutely true as Chris had bought me a beautiful green lace agate pendant shortly before her passing, proving yet again just how close to us those in the spiritual world are, and how they go to great lengths endeavouring to convey messages of comfort and reassurance of there really being an after-life after our short journey on the earth plane comes to a conclusion.

Our mind has several energy consciousness states including the conscious logical mind, the subconscious mind which records and memorises every single event that has happened throughout our lives and processes millions of pieces of information per second, and the higher state of consciousness (or bliss state) which can elevate us by the power of thought into the spiritual realm.

Thought can, in fact, help us tremendously in creating our lives. For instance, if we hold continual negative thoughts of illness then they can manifest within our physical body. However, if we think thoughts of good health, happiness and success then these thought forms filter through our subconscious and bring much welcome positive change to our everyday lives.

Meditation is a wonderful way of contacting the spirit world and can also help in alleviating much stress and strain from our everyday lives, but firstly we have to quieten the chatter of our minds and raise our level of mind consciousness to reach out to the spiritual dimension. There are many ways of relaxation. I have found one of the easiest methods being to just sit comfortably, close our eyes and slowly breathe in to the count of four, hold the breath to the count of three and thereafter exhale, again to the count of four; continue doing this a few times and then relax.

There are several ways of meditating after completing the relaxation technique above such as focusing our eyes on a candle flame for two or three minutes, or just concentrate on our breathing for several minutes, or listen to a guided meditation – it is just a question of finding out what method suits. Approximately twenty minutes each day in a quiet undisturbed place will help in opening up to spirit, but always remember the closing down or grounding technique afterwards, i.e. imagine a golden light surrounding your body then slowly breathe the light into each energy centre (or chakra) from head to toe to close that centre, or just stamping your feet on the ground beneath you will help to connect with the earth energy once again.

In December 2012 I was again preparing to go to see my brother and sister-in-law in Nottingham when to my amazement their close late friend Roy whom had passed to the Other Side with a cancer condition suddenly manifested in front of me looking very fit and happy. I had not known him that well and did not understand why he had come through to me when I heard him start to relay telepathically his interest in photography and his special camera. He spoke about his wife and 'Gran Canaria' and said how important his family was to him, repeatedly mentioning his own brother, all of whom were still on the earth plane. Upon my arrival in Nottingham I told my brother and sister-in-law about the amazing occurrence when my sister-in-law immediately informed me that the camera Roy had mentioned was, in fact, the one she had previously given to me as a gift soon after his passing into spirit, and also that his wife had just returned from holidaying in the Canary Islands! Also, Roy's brother had sadly just had a very serious health scare only a few weeks ago! I then realised the reason for my visit at that particular time to my brother and sister-in-law was perhaps to comfortingly reassure Roy's wife and family that he was, indeed, very much 'alive and kicking' on the Other Side and thinking of his beloved family here on the earth plane.

There was one phenomenal and unforgettable spiritual sighting that will always remain with me which happened in the early afternoon of April 14th one Easter Sunday. It was just after two p.m. whilst I was relaxing at home in my upstairs bedroom when I began to feel an inexplicable sense of calm and peace. I then could hardly believe my eyes as a vivid blue mist suddenly began to envelop the whole atmosphere and immediately thought that this could perhaps be an exceptional spiritual energy endeavouring to make contact for some unknown reason. At that moment I was then completely and utterly in awe as standing right at the end of my bed smiling and looking very regal was no less than our late Princess Diana! I was speechless to see such an iconic figure when she began telepathically saying, "Just call me Diana!" She then stated that she often visited her ancestral home, Althorpe, with her late father, and also how happy and proud she was of her boys, William and Harry. She said that she had accompanied William, Kate and her grandson, George on their New Zealand and Australian trip, adding that their girls will be beautiful! Princess Diana stated how we change after crossing over into the spiritual dimension adding how vast it was and that there were many different energy levels. I then haltingly asked what did actually happen at her time of passing and the reason why she had been taken at such an early age to which she replied, "It had been a collaboration and it was my time to go!"

Princess Diana then continued to speak telepathically about her previous lifetime as Queen Isabella, daughter of the King of France, but suddenly the swirling blue mist that had enveloped my bedroom began to lift and she gradually began to recede into the atmosphere, at which point I just sat there in a state of shock and amazement at this truly incredible spiritual sighting.

I later decided to find out more about Queen Isabella and discovered that she had married the English king, Edward II in 1308 and had borne four children, but tragically he was deposed and murdered after a two-year reign with accusations of homosexuality tendencies surrounding him. However, prior to Edward's assassination Isabella had desperately fallen in love with a Roger Mortimer, managing to move to France with him, only to return to England in 1326; Edward was deposed in 1327 in favour of his fourteen-year-old son and Isabella and

Roger Mortimer ruled in his name until 1330 when Edward III seized power and Mortimer was executed forcing Isabella to retire completely from public life.

Upon reflection, perhaps there was a karmic link between these possible two incarnations of our Princess Diana with certain spiritual lessons to be resolved. Who knows? However, one thing is certain, that I will never forget such a truly amazing and humbling unexpected spiritual manifestation.

All living creatures on the earth plane possess energy bodies and souls including our animal kingdom who also travel on into the vast spiritual dimension once their earthly journey is complete. Animals have always been a high priority in my family, a diverse array of dogs, cats, tortoise, fish, etc. having become beloved family members bringing forth the double-edged sword of immense joy and pleasure to the deepest of sorrow at their time of passing into spirit.

Many years ago whilst out walking near my home, I continuously found a plethora of small, white, plastic crosses at my feet and one particular afternoon whilst admiring the clear blue late summer sky I astonishingly could see an enormous white cross right above my house, which I immediately sensed was some kind of spiritual warning, although was at a loss as to its actual meaning. However, I was soon to discover the answer when not long after a much-loved tortoise-shell cat named Molly whom had been a family pet since a kitten suddenly passed into spirit, hence the loving spirit warnings of the crosses.

Molly was an old spiritual soul and always seemed to understand exactly how I felt, in fact I sensed she was, indeed, a soul mate and that we had possibly shared many incarnations together. On the day of her passing I was naturally grief-stricken, but drew some comfort at there being another beloved cat to focus on at home called Simmy who was a large, independent and fearless loving soul. Throughout that same evening I just sat at the foot of my hallway stairs crying endlessly at Molly's departure when brave Simmy suddenly dashed toward me looking up at the stairs, her eyes wide open and fur standing on end. She then hid behind the banister gingerly peeping out toward the centre of the stairs continuously turning round as though urging me to see what she was witnessing. I then began to tingle all over and instantly intuitively knew that it was Molly who had somehow found her way through the ether to comfort me and let me know that she was, indeed, very much alive in the spiritual dimension, showing just how caring and loving the souls of our animal kingdom truly are.

More convincing evidence of a spiritual animal kingdom was presented to me by way of a very old affectionate black cat named Reg who appeared at my doorstep one evening whom I later discovered had lived with a local family for nearly eleven years but had inexplicably decided to change his residence, even after much cajoling by his owners and myself to return home, but to no avail. He was a determined and loving old soul with a long bony physique and had apparently managed to survive a car smash which had resulted in his jaw being broken, teeth knocked out and having to be drip-fed for many months, but only to startlingly bounce back from all his injuries and make an astounding recovery. For the next three years I cared for Reg showering him with much love and attention and one quiet sunny spring-time morning decided to take a few photos of him with my old-fashioned camera while he was sitting quietly alone in my back garden. Reg obliging stared into the camera whilst I happily clicked away also taking advantage of such a beautiful warm day. The camera film was later developed in a local shop but whilst there I was suddenly ushered aside by the owner who proceeded to ask several questions about the animal in the photos explaining that when developing the photos he had experienced an icy cold feeling and a tingling sensation all through his arms. Upon looking at the pictures I was shocked as there draped across Reg's back was a strange looking creature with grey coloured fur (Reg was so thin and weak that he was incapable of carrying anything let alone another animal on his poor old back!). There also appeared to be a long tail positioned over his head and what looked like another cat's white claw on his right side which was somewhat puzzling, as without a shadow of doubt, only Reg and myself were in the garden at the time of the photo shoot

Sadly, two weeks after the photos were taken poor old Reg suddenly passed into the spirit world making me think that perhaps the strange phenomena in the photos were perhaps animal spirits gathering around in preparation for his imminent departure. Some days later I spoke to a well-known psychic and good friend called Shirley Jones showing her Reg's garden photos. She immediately stated there were the energies of animals present who had been helping him prepare for his departure which showed me again how very close the spiritual realm is.

Many years ago, I attended a Psychic College in Kingston-Upon-Thames, Surrey and sitting in one of the classes was an elderly gentleman who had been a pathologist in a prominent London governmental department for thirty years gradually climbing up the career ladder to become Head of the Pathology Department. He stated that he was attending the Psychic College because of the continuous inexplicable events that he and the pathology staff had witnessed over the years, which he added had unnerved everyone concerned and that he just wanted to find out more about what they had all witnessed. The retired pathologist mentioned his work had eerily involved working on many corpses in an endeavour to discover the exact cause of death and that intriguingly he and his staff had frequently observed a mysterious white mist arising from each body before fading slowly into the atmosphere. He had reported the sightings many, many times to his superior officers but was always forbidden to mention anything about them outside of the department with no explanation at all as to the reason for the secrecy.

The pathologist went on to describe one particularly startling sight which had unnerved him that had occurred after he had worked on the corpse of a young female who had tragically lost her life in a car accident. After working on the body he was driving home late that evening but after approximately twenty minutes he began to feel icily cold and happened to look into his rear view mirror when to his utter amazement saw the very same young girl sitting in the back seat smiling and dressed in exactly the same clothing that she had worn when brought into the Pathology Department. He was, naturally, very shocked and extremely shaken by this and, thankfully, managed to pull into a nearby lay-by where he just sat for over an hour trying to compose himself, but upon managing to force himself a little later to look again into his rear view mirror the young female had mysteriously vanished into thin air. He then slowly managed to drive home still in complete shock at what he had witnessed. Hence his visit to the local Psychic College to find out more about the white mist that had continuously been seen throughout his pathology career and also to explore more of the possibility of the existence of an after-life.

As previously mentioned, spiritual signs are shown to us in many different guises, such as butterflies that draw close, which can also be a sign of personal transformation. They have unexpectedly made their presence known to me on two separate occasions, one being during the summer of 2013. It was an unusually hot sultry July afternoon and as I was sitting in my back garden surrounded by summer-time pink and cream-coloured rose bushes, my two sleepy cats at my feet and magpies chattering away in an overhanging tree, the atmosphere suddenly became unusually quiet and the birds became silent, both my drowsy cats suddenly awakening from their slumber and peering around in all directions for some unknown reason. Within seconds two large white butterflies appeared from nowhere and began encircling my head for several minutes only to then completely vanish into the distant horizon. I immediately intuitively sensed that this could be a symbolic spiritual sign of possible new beginnings that I secretly hoped would involve my very first book being accepted by a publisher. This indeed turned out to be the case, as soon after I received the long-awaited news that my book had, in fact, finally been accepted by a well- known reputable publisher.

Another spiritual sign involving butterflies happened two months later while I was strolling along a quiet local leafy lane one evening, the daytime wildlife seemingly having retired to bed. I was in somewhat of a reflective mood thinking about beloved family members who had passed into spirit when out of the blue an enormous white butterfly appeared from nowhere, and again, began encircling my head before disappearing into the atmosphere. I then started to feel great warmth throughout my body and could telepathically hear the voice of my late father slowly relating a saying that he had sometimes used and which I had completely forgotten. "Do it now and stop procrastinating, life is short." It was wonderful to hear his voice again and know that he was so close to me although did not fully understand why he was relating this message, but sensed that it was possibly to do with a move of house that I had contemplated for several years, having procrastinated and not ever actually done anything about!

Some months later a beloved pet had recently undergone urgent medical treatment, which sadly resulted in her untimely passing into spirit, although I had desperately approached every available avenue at preventing her death. I was bereft and a week later was presented with an inordinate veterinary bill which was an impossibility for me to pay at that time. I lay tossing and turning in bed late into the night endeavouring to find a solution to the problem at which point I begged spirit for any help they could give. Several hours later and still unable to sleep I was startled to see the figure of my late father standing at the end of the bed dressed in familiar shirt and trousers that he often wore whilst on the earth plane, but did not recognize the other energy with him who was dressed completely in black with a large brimmed hat perched on his head. My father then began to telepathically relay a message of love and encouragement, although the other man's stern message advised me not to interfere with the natural laws of nature when it is our time to pass into spirit, including those from the animal kingdom; I presumed by his warning that he was referring to my unsuccessful desperate attempt to clinically prolong my pet's life. The apparitions then slowly began to fade into the atmosphere leaving me with a sense of both hope for the future and guidance to always remember our laws of nature, especially where the animal fraternity are concerned.

One week later I was invited to a local entertainment venue where a lottery was being held with various prizes being offered from household goods to a continental holiday and also a prize of £500. Hundreds of people flocked to attend the event and purchase tickets, including myself, and towards the end of the evening I was overjoyed to learn that my one ticket had amazingly been selected to win the main prize of the night! I was ecstatic, especially with the aforementioned, large veterinary bill looming over my head. As I left the venue to return home upon reaching the nearby train station I happened to glance over to the opposite platform and there was a cream-coloured poster displaying in large black lettering the words, JOHN GREEN WITH LOVE, which I presumed was advertising perhaps a new book. However, I immediately sensed that this was personal confirmation of my late father's loving intervention in helping me with the veterinary bill, especially as my paternal family name is JOHN GREEN, my father being WILLIAM JOHN GREEN!

The month of June 2014 brought yet another distressing sad circumstance when a beloved lively cat of mine was mysteriously struck down by an unknown virus. It was heart-breaking to watch her feebly endeavouring to move and again, in desperation, I turned to spirit for help, although bearing in mind spirit's prior unforgettable warning not to interfere with the laws of nature!

However, to my utter surprise the very next day several local neighbours unexpectedly rallied around after hearing of my plight and guided me to one of the most caring individuals I have ever come across called Simon who just happened to be a local vet. He went out of his way to administer continuous loving care to my sick animal, even coming to her rescue when she had quietly crept away without my knowledge managing to become wedged between two garages at the rear of my home. Simon never once left my cat's side, even attending to her in the middle of the night at his surgery. Thankfully, my beloved cat survived her traumatic ordeal, which I knew in hindsight was the result of Simon and the local community, and whom I also intuitively felt were 'earth angels' sent in my hour of need, who are often guided toward us in times of dire distress.

Several weeks later I received the veterinary fee which had, in fact, been substantially reduced but panic set in once again as to how I could find the funds. I decided once more to beg spirit for help and amazingly their response came the very next week when I unexpectedly won a local competition, the prize being £300, which left me in awe and gratitude at just how caring and loving the spiritual realm are. As long as we remember to ask spirit for help, our requests are always heard and answered for the good of all concerned, no matter what the situation.

My late father was an old soul, far ahead of his time, and one of the wisest individuals I have ever known. He was an extremely logical and level-headed individual, always holding the strong belief of there being a multitude of energy planes far beyond our own planet. He also strongly believed in there being an eternal life cycle and our unquestionable connection to the kingdom of nature i.e. our illuminating, blossoming and extinguishing and re-igniting for further incarnations. He was a down to earth individual who did not suffer fools gladly, displaying a certain scepticism for what he regarded as 'tall stories'. There was one memorable occasion which happened one

October night shortly before he passed into spirit whilst he was out walking his beloved black retriever Lucky. As he sauntered through the nearby quiet, undisturbed farmland reflecting on his somewhat challenging life since childhood and pondering on what might lay ahead he suddenly heard a clear, deep, echoing voice within his ear stating, "I am with you always." He immediately looked all about him but could not see anybody-else near to him and just stood there for several minutes in complete and utter amazement at what he had just heard, sensing a tremendous calmness throughout his entire body at that moment and realising that we are, indeed, not alone, whichever lifetime we are experiencing.

Another illustration of spiritual love and assurance took place in a white brick care home set in a tree-lined avenue surrounded by wide green lawns and colourful flowers where my ninety-six-year-old Uncle Vic resided. He was number three in a family of six boisterous boys. He had, like my late father, quite literally pulled himself up by his boot-strings as life had been challenging since an early age having lost his adored mother at just forty-one years of age, and having to work since a young boy, including tending his father's numerous allotments ensuring that all the family had their daily quota of fruit and vegetables

Uncle Vic, like many of his generation, was a courageous and brave soul having completed his National Service even after becoming a prisoner in

North Africa for several years until the end of World War II, only to be released and later become the proud owner of a large construction company in South West London. He later met and married a vivacious petite lady called Joy and they travelled the world together enjoying in his later life the fruits of his hard-earned pounds, shillings and pence. However, his adored wife passed into spirit from cancer at just fifty-one years of age, but he soldiered on alone until spending his last years in the aforementioned care home in Surbiton where he lived to the grand old age of ninety-eight. Uncle Vic luckily still had all his mental faculties whilst in care and often spoke affectionately of his five brothers, four of whom had sadly passed into spirit many years before. I often used to visit him and one summer afternoon we were sitting relaxing and reminiscing about his earlier life when he unexpectedly kept mentioning his brother, Ernie, who had emigrated to Australia seeking his fortune by opal digging in the mines of Southern Australia, but whose hopes were sadly dashed when his dreams did not come to fruition, eventually passing away in his eighties sitting in the Australian sunshine surrounded by his beloved family and favourite lemon trees!

Uncle Vic continued speaking of his brother, Ernie, for the rest of the afternoon forever reiterating melancholy how he would 'give a million pounds' to see him once again when suddenly he appeared to become very unusually agitated frequently turning around and looking over his left shoulder stating, "Who keeps prodding me? Who is it?" (I would mention that there was no one else in the quiet corner where we were sitting at the time.) My uncle was, as stated, mentally very alert, and a somewhat gruff, logical individual who did not suffer fools gladly and was certainly not in the habit of making anything up that was untrue. He then looked at me demanding to know who it was that was playing tricks on him, but again, there were only the two of us sitting there. However, I instantly intuitively sensed that old Uncle Ernie had probably come to pay us an unexpected visit after hearing of his brother's affectionate plea in the hope of perhaps endeavouring to reassure him that he was close and there was indeed, life after physical death. However, I somehow sensed that my Uncle Vic would possibly not have shared that same opinion in spite of his brother's loving efforts to reassure him!

Many years ago, there was a very sad child abuse case which tragically resulted in his death. The case created a huge well of national grief after much publicity in the national press. I was deeply disturbed at what the poor baby had suffered, and like many others, decided to pay my respects and visit the poor mite's grave situated in a large London cemetery. Upon arrival I was taken aback at the vastness of the place and later learnt that it was, in fact, the largest of its kind in the London area. I proceeded to follow the directions of a security guard at one of the main entry gates, but then seemed to be walking endlessly up and down a multitude of pathways strewn with all manner of colourful flowers, before realising hours later that I had probably walked for miles and completely off the beaten track, even thinking that I might have to camp down for the night there as my mobile phone was not working and eerily there was not a soul around, in spite of the size of the graveyard.

I silently said a prayer and out of the blue I suddenly detected a woman ahead of me who appeared to be smiling and beckoning me to approach her. I felt a huge sense of relief as I walked toward her but upon reaching her noticed there was something quite unusual about the lady's facial features and extraordinary piercing icy-blue eyes which unnerved me. She seemingly had a quiet manner about her and just uttered one word, 'come' beckoning me to follow her. I then endeavoured to explain the purpose of my visit, but she did not say another word, although I felt that the calmness surrounding her was all-consuming.

She then directed me toward the grave where I wanted to pay my respects and I then laid a large bunch of pink and yellow roses amongst a mountain of wreaths and tributes already there.

After staying for several minutes I turned to go, only to discover that the strange lady mentioned above had been waiting for me and once again beckoned me to follow her, but without uttering a word and what seemed even stranger, was the fact that we still appeared to be the only people in the vast cemetery.

As we finally arrived at one of the main entrances, I looked for directions to the local train station and upon turning to thank the woman in question she had mysteriously vanished from sight without saying a single word. When I finally arrived home and reflected upon the unusual events of that afternoon. I felt with great affection that spirit had once again sent an earth angel to me in my hour of need.

The spiritual realm do help us all in so many different ways and confirmation of this happened yet again one late evening in January 2014 when I was sitting at home alone and feeling a sense of fearfulness and anxiety for no particular reason. I decided to ask spirit for help at which point I felt an urge to switch my radio on when I instantly heard a voice stating firmly, "If there are any of you listening out there feeling worried, fearful and insecure, I would like to give you some hope and guidance." I presumed that I had inadvertently tuned into a station unfamiliar to me, but then proceeded to hear, "Those negative thoughts will attract the same," continuing to quote the biblical story of David and Goliath to gather strength within and alleviate all fear, also stating how loving and protective the spiritual realm is and the closeness of their energy dimension. I was astounded and immediately sensed that this was spirit's loving message of reassurance and comfort, immediately sending up a silent prayer for their instantaneous loving care and guidance.

Another meeting with an earth angel occurred one bleak January day after I had arranged to give a psychic reading to a new client in an unfamiliar area of London. Upon leaving her home, dusk was beginning to settle and transport appeared to be very scanty so I began searching for directions to the nearest tube station where my coach home would be, but alas without success. I was by then becoming more and more alarmed when out of the blue I heard an extremely calming voice saying, "I am here to help, do not worry."

I turned around to discover a tall, fair-haired gentleman who appeared to radiate an indescribable sense of peace and who could only be described as ethereal, gesturing me to follow and constantly uttering, "Come." It is not within my nature to follow a complete stranger but I then found myself dutifully walking at his side where he weaved us in and out of the crowded streets, reiterating quietly that he was here to help and protect, all the while giving out an unfathomable sense of utter calm and peace within me. With great relief we arrived at my destination and I turned to thank him profusely, only to discover he had completely disappeared into the bustling crowd without saying a word of goodbye. It was at that very moment that I realised the extraordinary resemblance to the previous earth angel mentioned and could only think again just how loving and protective spirit really are in our hour of need.

However, the story did not end there as throughout my homeward-bound coach journey I was startled to see through its front panoramic windows a huge shimmering white cross in the sky until the coach neared my home town when I noticed it slowly begin to disintegrate into the night sky. On reflection the following day of the fascinating trail of events I intuitively sensed the utter love and care the spiritual dimension project and this was certainly one instance that will always remain in my memory.

Further evidence of life after physical death occurred many centuries ago in 1891 in Iowa in the U.S.A. when a local farmer was tragically found dead one evening on his farm. Upon discovering his body workmates carried him to the local morgue where his corpse was attended to and his dirty working clothes were removed and his body then prepared for return to his home. His son collected his father's corpse and began relaying the tragic news to his sister awaiting their arrival. She immediately requested to see his body and thereafter began to somewhat hysterically state that her father had puzzlingly just appeared to her dressed in a white shirt, black trousers and his comfortable old slippers, also mentioning that he had sewed a large roll of money inside his grey shirt, including a cutting from her red dress, adding that the money was still there. The very next day she and her brother travelled back to the morgue and luckily managed to retrieve their father's clothes only to find the roll of notes sewn into his shirt with the article of red cloth from his daughter's dress exactly as he had told her when he had mysteriously appeared to her.

A famous and well-loved disc jockey by the name of Ray Moore sadly passed into spirit in the early 1990s with a terminal cancer condition. Prior to his passing, he had desperately turned to a reputable healer for help and whilst he was speaking to her on the telephone his late father began to communicate with the healer from the Other Side relaying personal information about Ray which the healer could not possibly have known. During his first healing session Ray told the healer that every bit of the information she had relayed to him had been astoundingly accurate, also mentioning that several hands were felt as the healing continued, although there were only the two of them present!

The healing helped Ray enormously emotionally and gave him great comfort, in spite of the fact that he was called into spirit at a much later date.

91

Chapter Seven

Ancient Natural Laws

There are numerous ancient natural universal laws which have existed since time began from the much publicized Law of Attraction, the Law of Cause and Effect (i.e. what comes around goes around), the Law of Gratitude and the Law of Grace, which many great people throughout the ages have been aware of and the spiritual lessons, including purity of heart and mind, which continuously lead us to a higher level of knowledge and evolvement.

Our mind energy is a powerful asset and can create the life we lead; the subconscious part stores memories of every single incident that has happened to us throughout our lifetime and deals with everyday matters, whilst the conscious part is our more logical side. All energy has a frequency and is determined by our thoughts, i.e. whatever we focus on, for example, from health to wealth, then that particular thought energy will be delivered to us, as every thought is a powerful energy form.

We can change our life by the power of our thoughts even where disease is concerned. There is a well-known story relating to a famed author, Morris Goodman, who had a life threatening accident when he crashed an aeroplane in March 1981 and suffered spinal cord injuries, vertebrae breakage and his swallowing reflex was totally destroyed, together with his diaphragm, resulting in his being unable to eat, drink or hardly breathe. He was completely paralysed and was told that he would be a vegetable for the rest of his life. However, Morris was already well aware of the power of mind energy and knew that this was all he had left to repair his broken body, so he slowly began to visualise himself getting better and better and actually being able to walk out of the hospital the following Christmas, although all the medical staff said nothing could be done. However, he relentlessly believed that we become what we think about and against all the odds, finally walked out of the hospital unaided, giving thousands and thousands of people worldwide inspiration and knowledge of just how powerful our mind energy truly is.

The Law of Attraction is one of the most famed of the universal natural laws, i.e. like attracts like, especially where thoughts are concerned and has been used for countless reasons from success to happiness and wealth etc. Thinking continuous thoughts of abundance is what brings wealth to many and not allowing any negativity to counteract their mind energy as this law will always respond to our thoughts whatever they might be, i.e. our dominant thoughts will always bring those thoughts to actual fruition, whether positive or negative. Thoughts are magnetic and what we think the universe will boomerang back that energy to us as every thought has a differing frequency; always think of what you want, not what you don't want because, as mentioned, the Law of Attraction does not distinguish between positive or negative energy, so continuously thinking abundance, for instance, will attract that same energy toward us, as with all the plethora of other natural ancient laws.

Chapter Eight

Our Soul's Survival

Miracles manifest in so many different ways from the creation of our magnificent universe to actual life itself with both a physical and an etheric energy body and an attaching energy cord that only breaks away at the time of physical death. Throughout my psychic journey I have astonishingly learnt that our soul, or spirit, housed within our etheric energy body continues to evolve throughout many lifetimes, which is a realm of thought where our physical earthly necessities such as eating, drinking, sleeping etc, are not needed. When spirit make contact with us they are sometimes dressed in similar apparel to what they wore on the earth plane, as even this is comprised of thought on the Other Side, i.e. every thought is an energy.

When our energy body housing our soul crosses into the spiritual realm and our physical body is no longer required all our earthly thoughts go with us as thought forms are eternal, and as mentioned, the spiritual dimension is a world of thought and our soul, or spirit, will now reside where materialism is no longer needed. Eating, sleeping, working, etc. is not necessary because of the enormity of thought in the spiritual realm, and it is always quite a shock for those who pass over to come to terms with the enormous differences between our two energy planes.

Our surrounding etheric energy body has several layers, the astral being where we travel onto once our earthly journey is complete; the inhabitants of the astral plane resemble their earthly bodies and also can vary their length of stay on that energy dimension before moving onto higher planes, or even return to earth in order to resolve any new spiritual lessons. Each layer of our surrounding etheric body vibrates at a different frequency, the lowest density being our earth energy and the higher, finer layers beyond the astral are connected to the Universal Energy consciousness, or God energy, the highest level of which is known as the celestial. I have humbly learnt that there are higher souls who exist on the astral known as ascended masters and guides who have lived on the earth plane at some point, and also angels who have never lived on our planet. Mediums and sometimes psychics usually make communication via the astral energy plane although they can also communicate with higher dimensions.

Once our earthly journey is finished we travel on toward the energy planes which will benefit our soul, or spirit, which very much depends upon the kind of life that we have led whilst on the earth plane. The soul enters our world to learn, and each and every part of our earthly journey is an opportunity for it to evolve i.e. our place is earned in the spiritual realm according to the life that we have lived whilst on the earth plane and from which our soul grows. If we have led an earthly life causing pain and suffering to others then we do unintentionally create our own heaven or hell, although I believe that hell does not exist, but is just a cold and bleak misty part of the astral dimension. Many people are reminded of their positive and negative times whilst on earth, even if suffering to others has been caused, and then a remorseful period is undertaken by the soul on the Other Side.

I have humbly learnt that we live many, many lifetimes and are born into the life that we have earned in previous incarnations. Our soul will be housed in a physical body to learn and grow from the positive and negative actions we undertake during our earthly lifetimes, and evolves throughout the varying energy levels on the Other Side, although some souls choose to return to the earth plane to complete unfinished spiritual lessons before progressing onto the next energy dimension.

In conclusion, I have also humbly learnt throughout my earthly lifetime that every incarnation is but a short moment in time and a true learning platform before our re-birth into the vast energy planes of the spiritual realm where our evolvement truly begins and where we all meet again, free of earthly physical and mental challenges. This, I hope, will give some comfort to those who may be soldiering on through their darkest of hours, and even those who might be pondering what, if anything, might lay ahead once their earthly journey is complete.

A Recipe for Life

Sunshine and showers stirred into
the mix, forever what makes
life tick. Beauty and riches
being all very well, but 'tis
good health, love and
laughter what sell.

Hopes and dreams always on
offer guide the way for
a better tomorro'.

Faith helps conquer sorrow
and fear even when shedding
the unexpected tear. In sensing
that we are never alone
gives much comfort in knowing
our true eternal home.

Health

*Good health, the greatest gift
of all, neither earned nor
bought, only bestowed upon
the luckiest of all.*

*Ill health is but a cruel disease
robbing us of our dignity,
striking all manner of creed
and class, never waiting to
be asked.*

*There but for the grace of God
go I as a lesser soul
passes me by. So let us
be kind to one another,
whatever our destiny imparts,
as 'tis well to remember
we are all one at the last
setting sun.*

A futuristic moment

Wisdom and knowledge forever
attained through life decades of
pains and gains.

The 21st century is, indeed, a
spectacular feat of ground-breaking
technology: Gene editing and stem
cell replenishing eradicates old age
extending life beyond the grave.

Robots stand alongside man
multi-tasking without asking.
Perhaps we may unsustain
and prepare for a
new galactic domain.

An undiscovered plateau per se
far beyond our milky way
where we might freely roam,
soon to frequent another
universal solar home.

Family

Parents

Earth Angels were there as
life was given, lovingly
guiding me through every
decision, our not always seeing
eye to eye, but forever encouraging
to reach for the sky.

My salvation, my strength, my
mother and father, heaven sent.

Grandmother, Amelia

Horseracing was nan's lifelong
passion, horses and jockeys never
on ration. Trotting along in her
pony and trap, fluttering lacy parasol
fixedly in her lap.

Jockeys' silks dancing in the breeze,
Derby Day was truly nan's
'bees knees'

Bookmakers shout their odds across
a muddy soil, magnificent open
carriages carry the precious Royals,
making their presence known to
loyal subjects, albeit unknown.

Sturdy steeds gallop at breakneck
speed, the winning post firmly
in sight, that cossetted prize
suddenly coming alive before
their very eyes, perhaps this year
will be their ultimate paradise.

Aunt Winnifred

Canny old Aunt Winn, sharp
as a shiny new pin, lythe
and slim was she, there's
no flies on me she decreed,
a vegan I'll always be.

Munching away on her apples
and pears, my could she
zip up them stairs.

Her 90-year-old frame stood
proudly in the rain ever
ready to withstand any pain
a-calling, struth what an
example she was to us all.

Sister-in-law Christine

Earthly life is but a moment
in time endeavouring to
teach us lessons in kind.

Our precious Christine, a beacon
of light, shining through the
darkest of nights.

Her kindness and loyalty knew
no bounds, forever helping those
around. Astounding bravery and
positivity never wavering, even when
facing the cruellest of adversity,
making for truly inspirational sound.

As dear Christine travels onto
the next energy plane, we
give thanks she is now free
of pain, and loo forward
to when we meet again.

Friends

Gill

Chirpy as a cricket
was our Gill, fun and
laughter always on the ticket.

Dancing away into the night,
ever ready to meet her
cherished 'Mr Right'.

Forever there to lend a
helping hand, never failing to
understand, her calming presence
like smooth silk sand.

Jim

Gentleman Jim sent my heart in
a spin: Just walking into
the room made my heart go
boom.

Courtship was only just a
game, but oh, for the
remedy that produced such
chemistry; I wonder, will
that ever come again?

But hey, ho, there's always
the next life I sigh
where I could even end up
Jim's 'trouble and strife'.
So here's to the next round
Gentleman Jim when we may
even come floatin' down agin'!

Youth

The dancing sprite of youth so bright
dancing and laughing far into
the night, brimming with untold
zest and vigour for a dream-laden
utopia as yet unseen.

Oh, to return to those carefree
salad days, just how did
they evaporate into the maze!

A Mid-Life Reflection

Peering into the mirror I cry
just who is that looking
me in the eye. It surely
must be a trick of the
light as yet another grey
hair sashays into sight.

This definitely is NOT my
cup of tea I decree,
why I'm only just a sprig
off the tree!

But hey, there's no time
for tears or regrets,
I'll just let gene therapy
be my new best friend and
party on right till the end.